40 days of Hope, Healing, and Love

YOU ARE

*Messages of Love to Encourage,
Empower, and Inspire*

Dr. Britt Elizabeth

Love Letters of the Divine

YOU ARE ~ 40 days of Hope, Healing, and Love. Messages of Love to Encourage, Empower, and Inspire.

© 2025 by Dr. Britt Elizabeth

Paperback ISBN: 979-8-9986391-0-4
Hardcover ISBN: 979-8-9986391-3-5
E-book ISBN: 979-8-9986391-1-1
Audiobook ISBN: 979-8-9986391-2-8
LCCN: 2025917127

All rights reserved. No portion of this book may be reproduced, distributed, stored in retrieval system, or transmitted in any form or by any means, electronic, mechanical, photocopy, recording, scanning, or other, without written permission from, or action by, the publisher or author, except in the case of brief quotations embodied in critical reviews, articles, and certain other noncommercial uses permitted by copyright law.

Please send requests and/or inquiries to lovelettersofthedivine@gmail.com

View other works by this author at www.drbrittelizabeth.com

First Edition
Series: You Are
Collection: Love Letters of the Divine

Authored and Published by: Dr. Britt Elizabeth
Cover Design and Illustration by: Dr. Britt Elizabeth
Photographs: iStock, Shutterstock, Pixabay

Dedication

This work is dedicated to YOU.

All who hold the line of goodness, faith, hope, and fierce love in this world.

The lovers.
The healers.
The believers.
The teachers.
The messengers.
The warriors.
The lightworkers.
The gap-standers.
The change-makers.
The truth-tellers.
The chain breakers.
The bridges.
The shepherds.
The peacekeepers.
The pure hearts.
The intercessors.
The light-bringers.
The seers.
The faithful.
The black sheep.
The underdogs.
The gentle.
The kind.
The heartbroken.
The merciful.
The misunderstood.

…and to my Isaac and Elijah, and all those we love, breathe, and fight for.

Contents

You are:

1. Brilliance
2. Steadfastness
3. Perseverance
4. Humility
5. Love
6. Bravery
7. Beauty
8. On Purpose
9. A Gift
10. Depth
11. Presence
12. Transcendence
13. Sacred
14. Meant to Shine
15. Light
16. Worthy of Care
17. Strength
18. A Beautiful Soul
19. A Miracle
20. A Safe Place
21. Mighty
22. Lovable
23. Glorious
24. Respite
25. Quirky
26. Growing
27. Mysterious
28. Different
29. A Beautiful Creation
30. Treasured
31. My Dearest
32. Magnificent
33. Courage
34. A Leader
35. Chosen
36. A Bridge
37. Prepared
38. Fierce
39. A Smile-Bringer
40. Called

Introduction

My dear friend,

I am deeply honored to share this work with you.

These messages have met me in my 40th year, after many long seasons in the wilderness. They have become my lifeline, and I pray they do for you as well.

May these love letters bring healing, miracles, and wonders to your world. May the hands of the greatest healer cradle your soul, mend your heart and body, and bring peace to your mind. May you be encouraged and awoken to the gifts awaiting bloom within you. This world needs you and all you were made to be.

Some messages are direct and others come through as metaphors, analogies, and/or visions. These are the ways in which the Holy Spirit speaks to me, sometimes edifying, but always in a tone of love and gentleness, admiration, inspiration, and encouragement. I share these messages with you as was received and led.

Please prepare yourself to receive this outpouring. Soften your heart. Lower your walls, or carve out a few windows, even if only for a moment. Breathe it all in. Let love walk you home…and know, this is for you, you who shine light in the darkest of places so that others may see. Be encouraged as our stories unfold together.

With Love and Gratitude,

You are
Brilliance #1

Of a great brightness, elegance, luster, and/or magnificence.

You are Brilliance

My precious one, you are the beauty that is the morning sun. You are the warmth that touches faces and begs for people to outstretch their bare arms. You are vibrant and glowing in all the colors that touch the eyes, begging for it to be captured by the lens of permanence. Your essence shows colors only known, and seen, in Heaven.

Your brilliance is treasured. It isn't a luster meant to be dimmed. Please know the value of the gem that you are. Sweet one, don't let the mud of this world cloak your innate shine.

You are
Steadfastness #2

Firm in a purpose or path. Maintaining faith, resolute.

You are **Steadfastness**

My love, you are as the mountain erupted from the earth. You are steady and strong. You are not swayed by the breeze, or even the great shaking of the earth. You have snowy peaks and warm valleys. Your ancient stories, told through generations, are as the wise and gentle grand(father) of old who gathers the children upon his lap.

You are

Perseverance #3

Steady determination in a course of action, a purpose, especially in spite of difficulties.

You are **Perseverance**

You are the way of the water. The river that flows and finds its way, always...strong and mighty. It winds its way through the narrowest of gates...through the rock to forge mighty canyons. It finds its way to the most beautiful of lakes or mountain streams. Or it is called, beckoned, to join force in might with the great seas.

You are

Humility #4

Modest opinion of oneself or estimate of one's own importance, not pride or arrogance.

You are **Humility**

You are like the mighty tree of the forest. That which has seen generations seek shelter and a home under its branches. One that boasts an underground system connecting thousands of acres…and with a bloom that will take all breath away. It holds the great knowledge of the forest, the key to the connection of all below, the beauty, the life-sustaining breath…a cornerstone. Cloaked, however, are most to its great purpose and mightiness. It stands as a giant with the humility of the clover.

You are
Love #5

A deep feeling of personal attachment or profound affection, tender, having great concern for the well-being of another.

You are **Love**

Oh, my sweet child, how you are love. Your smile ignites hearts. Your warm embrace shatters coldness within. Your laughter shakes the belly of the downtrodden and mends the brokenhearted. I call you love, my dear sweet one, for you are the love and peace embodiment of my fruits, pulsating out into the world.

I am so proud of you. You are learning the way of the narrow path...not one of muddied perception, but one of love...one where each step is a check in with the heart-soul and with me who lives in you. Oh, my sweet one, how you yearn to heal others, to bring peace, joy, love...if only you knew how much you did that already. My sweet love, I will speak these words endlessly. You are love. You are loved.

You are

Bravery #6

Having a character of courage, valor, a willingness to press forward despite fear.

You are **Bravery**

You stand against the waves, strong one. You know you will be rolled, over and over, yet you rise. Your forehead is bruised and battered. Sand fills every crevasse. You grind it between your teeth. You are pained and uncomfortable, yet you rise. You meet each wave knowing it may knock you down, may batter you, may pull you out to sea...yet you rise and stand fast. How I stand, in amazement of you, my precious one.

You are

Beauty #7

The quality, grace, or charm giving deep satisfaction or pleasure in a thing or person.

You are **Beauty**

You are as beautiful as the morning dew. As it glimmers and shines in the morning sun, so do you. Its beautiful presence nourishes the grasses, flowers, and tree buds alike. It is a drink of life to the tiniest of creatures who begin and end the cycle of life. The beauty you behold is a forever beginning, there is no end to the ways in which your beauty illuminates and feeds all that surrounds it. It beckons, not in a lustful beauty, but in a way of bringing about goodness and expansive betterment. You, my beautiful one, anchor glorious joy into the darkness, yearning illumination.

You are

On Purpose #8

A reason by which something exists or is done, made, used, or on a certain path or trajectory.

You are On Purpose

You are not by accident!!!

I know you sometimes feel that you don't belong. Where an overwhelming sorrow of unbelonging has filled your bones since the very beginning. You were never meant to take on, or have that burden, little one. It's okay. Let the tears fall. The truth is, you are so very special…so very on purpose…one of understanding and a safe place meant to bring life and love, goodness, and joy to this world. There are no accidents, my sweet one, and even if there were, you surely, would never have been one. You are one of my most precious, beautiful, loved and special creations.

You are my bright light!!!

You are
A Gift #9

Something that is given without payment in return, as to show favor, honor an occasion, or as a gesture of care.

You are a **Gift**

You are the wisdom of old and the openness of the new. Your laughter wraps all around you in glittering goodness and your smile is the bow of gladness, joy, and love. You are so special to me, and I work all things for your good. I work in your favor, and for the favor of my children. You are meant to be that bridge, that light, that truth, that gap-stander. You are imperative. You are a catalyst. You are one I call 'love'. You are to be fully present for yourself. YOU ARE A GIFT!!!

You are

Depth #10

Copious intelligence, wisdom, insight,
and/or experience of a person.

You are **Depth**

Marianna's trench holds nothing in comparison to the depth of your soul. The waters in which your depth resides can support an eternal swim with no droplet touching the body twice. Drink it all up. Accept it. Trust the endless ocean in which your depth resides. Don't ever shallow, my love, that is not where you belong.

You are

Presence #11

The state or fact of being with others or in a place, or in a quality or manner of bearing in a status or current space.

You are **Presence**

Breathe in every moment. Every molecule. Cherish each touch, each memory... For it is not in the repetition of loss you've experienced, or its flashbacks, but in holding joy, love, peace...sensuality. Sensuality, not meant in the narrow term of physicality, but in living each moment, to take in the fragrance of the flower...to cherish every bud and every tiny insect that pollinates her. The softness of the petal, the fragility, the beauty...take in the colors that you've never noticed. Let all senses given to you for joy, enjoyment, love, knowledge, and wisdom be alive in presence...lap up each moment, and each miracle, found and kept in all things...

You are

Transcendence #12

Going beyond ordinary limits,
surpassing, exceeding.

You are **Transcendence**

Keep transcending my dear one, you are arising, becoming anew...while reborn of old. You walk with such beauty, such love, such joy, and now, you join that tenderness with ferocity. You love all, although sometimes with a sword against the darkness. Your gifts grow each day. My dear one, you are soft and beautiful, tender and true, loyal and loving. You are a kind, but fiercely loving protector. You, in tandem with your kin, will lead many in darkness to the light.

You are

Sacred #13

Connected to God, faith, or
religious doctrine.

You are **Sacred**

You are a sacred vessel of my love and light. Your makeup drips of my being, my love...the light which overtakes. Your purpose is profound. Your mission is majestic. Your time is coming, beloved. Stay fixed on my voice...my leading. Watch as your path is illuminated. Stand fast in loving faith, hope, and joy, sweet one.

You are

Meant to

Shine #14

To glow, glisten, sparkle, or to appear with brightness or clearness, with purpose.

You are **Meant to Shine**

You are meant to shine. To be brilliant. To roar with joy. To laugh wildly as a child. To ignite the stars with your smile. To dance on the fringes of understanding. To welcome the awakening rain. To swim the depths of all you are but not drown. To take on giants and rescue the little things. To love without limit…in grace, freedom, peace, and understanding. To have roots and wings. To be fire and water. To be soil and sky. To be laughter and tears. To be duality and unity…and all that is goodness.

You are

Light #15

Something that illuminates, creates visibility, a beacon.

You are **Light**

My precious one, how easy it is for you to see the light in others.
You see how the sunrise would be a little less bright without them,
how the stars would lose a bit of their starry wonder.

But my dear, if only you could see that in you, too.
If only you could see how you are that brilliant,
unrecognizable color in the sunset.

How the animals and insects buzz with delight when you are around.
How those you see the light in continue to shine because you have stayed.
How you were made for a special purpose, with a special spark,
one that sees the glory in all things, as I.

My dear one, oh how that glory is in you, too.
How you stain Heavenly cheeks when you see so
clearly the beauty in all things, except you.

Please remember, my sweet, it is you that I have sent for a mission only you can fulfill. You are so very loved. You have been called. You have been sent to love, oh to love. You've been sent to build bridges where other structure crumbles…where hope is scarce and where hands that have never been held can hold each other. You've been sent to stand in gaps that would swallow others.

Hold on, my dear one, hold on…you'll soon see.

You are

Worthy of Care #16

Deserving of merit, excellence, well-being,
love, and protection.

You are **Worthy of Care**

My joy, you are meant to be checked on, to be safe, to be loved, and to be held.

Gone are the days of pouring into those who would not provide for you a glass of water. Over are the moments of stripping your skin for those who would not lend a surplus garment. Cleaved no more are you to those who meant to see you buried instead of planted. My dear one, continue to be the light-bringer you are. Trust on.

Let others love you. Let them meet you. Let others help you to bloom. Let love in.

You are

Strength #17

The ability, courage, and/or determination to withstand hardship, adversity, or pressure. It is both a physical power and inner resilience.

You are **Strength**

Oh my angel, you are so very sweet, so very kind. Your beautiful heart comes through in the way that you grieve for others, even those whom you do not know. You are so strong. Please know there is strength in the "fragility" of breaking for another. This is the strength that brings people together, that leads armies, that truly heals. Strength like this is what truly matters. This is how masses heal, how populations find community, how the many find strength…in love, in light and in understanding.

You are a Beautiful Soul #18

One who radiates kindness, love, and compassion. Their actions and presence bring warmth, positivity, and inspiration.

You are a **Beautiful Soul**

It's okay to have anger, it needs to come out. It's okay if that anger helps aids in creation. A balance is needed. Soft, but fierce. Strong, but gentle. Passionate, but pure. Loving, but truth-telling. Dualities are needed as they bring greater unity.

In unity, in experience, in the peeling back, you don't simply gaze into self, but also to and for another, without judgement or shame, and with genuine care and intent...that, my precious one, is where true unconditional love comes in.

This does not mean you must be thrown in the mud, but you can leave footprints. Self-sacrifice and self-abandonment are no more. It is in holding space and the willingness to sit with another until they can stand...this is where love walks in.

Please continue to be the beautiful soul that you are. Your impact is ubiquitous.

You are
a Miracle #19

An extraordinary and often unexpected event that cannot be explained by natural or scientific laws.

You are a **Miracle**

My child, you are more gifted, more talented than you'll ever know. You are a masterpiece. Quit comparing yourself to others. Yes, others are also so skilled, so gifted, so amazing. But sweet one, I wish you could see within you, that you could glimpse what I see. You are extraordinary. You light up the night sky for many in the darkness. Continue to be faithful, and exactly who you are. I didn't give you skills of this world, I gave you gifts that are out of this world! Watch them come.

You are

A Safe Place #20

A space, physical or emotional, where one feels accepted, and free to express themselves without fear of harm, judgment, or danger.

You are a Safe Place

This world needs greatly the arms of the safe places. It is in need of bridge-builders, gap-standers, those who don't have to understand it all, but can have love anyway...those who have been through the fire but stand strong on the other side for those still walking through it. Those who aid in the back burn, bring buckets of water, or risk being set ablaze by reaching in the fire for others. This world needs those who stand fast. Those who outstretch their hand. The world needs those who are brave enough to walk a path that others haven't, a path that doesn't align perfectly with others, a path that intersects, but is not linear. This world needs you, and those like you. It is in need of those who love without question, who give love and grace. Sweet one, the world needs you. The world is better with you. The world has so much more light with you in it. Hold fast. Stay strong. Know that good days are coming. You are needed as a beacon, a lighthouse, as one who holds the lamp. I need you to be one who helps light the way of truth, of goodness, of joy, of love, of peace, gentleness, and self-control. Of all of the things that my love is, you are here to infuse that great and beautiful love. I need you, they need you, dear one.

You are

Mighty #21

Great strength, power, or influence. Something or someone with impressive presence, resilience, and/or capability.

You are Mighty

You are a child of the Most High. You are loved beyond measure. I am so very proud of you, my overcomer. You are learning to thrive on being misunderstood. Misunderstanding brings about curiosity, growth, and eventually, understanding.

You are a bridge, honey. You are love. You are the hand-holder and the trusted of the rocks. You are the peak and the valley, you may be small in stature but have faith to move mountains. You are mighty, so very mighty. Please see all you are.

You are

Lovable #22

Worthy of being endeared and shown
warmth, kindness, and care.

You are **Lovable**

My dear one, your soft heart was molded in the palm of my hand, and oh what a precious heart it is. One that loves deeply despite the arrows that have pierced it, a true gift to this world. It is big and beautiful and has always loved others well. A heart that has continued to bleed for those often unappreciative of that big love. Those who, over many years, manipulated your mind into believing it was unworthy of love, and at times, living, and that is the greatest tragedy of all.

Stay, my great love, stay.

My cherished one, you are meant to be loved without abandon, including of self. The love you carry is a blend all your own, given by you alone. Better days are coming, including the many who truly support your fierce and passionate love. Sweetheart, it is time for you to be safe. You don't have to run or hide away, you can trust those parts of you that hear my voice, sweet one. Let them love you.

You are

Glorious #23

Magnificent, excellent, awe-inspiring,
worthy of admiration, and splendor.

You are **Glorious**

Your ability to heal and bring peace are glorious. That gloriousness in the rising of the sun, that place where daylight breaks and brings about the celebrated need of the day, the color, the warmth, the food and miracles that come with the sun.

My dear child, you cannot fail. You are rooted in me. You are mine. You lack nothing. You are the soft, warm wind that encircles and walks others home.

You are

Respite #24

A moment of rest and recovery, or temporary relief
or break from hardship, stress, or difficulty.

You are **Respite**

My dear one, you are here to do many things, but love has always been at the center. Your mission is love. It is bravely holding the line for others in the fire, although you often burned alone. Despite the skin you've given, you are a garment of protective love for others. You are safety. You are respite. You are peace.

My love, you give voice, and hope, to many even as you cry silent tears. Don't you see? I have never left you. You may have experienced a lifetime of battle, but my wings never stopped shielding you. My dear one, that is why you've been sent.

You've been battered and bruised, shackled, and cast aside, yet you stand. Take your place among the warriors and anchor the goodness, peace, and love in this world. Use the boulders hurled at you as a place of rest for the weary. Despite it all, you are a safe, trusted respite for the downtrodden. Your shoulders are a perch for many, but oh my sweet one, how precious, rare, and gently held you are in the palm of my hand. You are cherished and softly nursed, of the mother's love, willing to give up her life for her young.

You are

Quirky #25

Unconventional, playful, or
uniquely different.

You are **Quirky**

I know, quirky…is that a compliment?

The truth is, dear one, you are quirky. You are unique and exactly who I made you to be. You have that laugh. Sure, some may roll their eyes, but you weren't made for them. That laugh…it brings joy, six-pack abs, and a chorus of cackles to so many. Did you know, my sweet one, that laughter really does heal?

Where would you be without the traits that make you, you? My sweet one, you were not made to fit in, but to stand out. You can try to blend in amongst the herd, but your stripes will always give you away. You were meant to stand out, not stand in.

My dear, your quirks were never mistakes, they were your finishing touches.

YOU ARE ~ 40 days of Hope, Healing, and Love. Messages of Love to Encourage, Empower, and Inspire.

You are
Growing #26

The process of evolution, development,
and improvement.

You are Growing

Oh my dear one, how you eclipse the darkness of a place or of a space. Your brain, your words, your heart, your soul, your very being is a gift. At some point you're going to believe that.

You feel as if you're still standing on the beach with sand up to your neck. The truth is, though, you're already in the middle of the ocean…a safe, loving ocean, with limitless potential, resources, and new lands of discovery. You are, and have been, growing. What you don't see yet is how many others you're inspiring to join you, that is where it's all at. It is your ability to pour into others despite a physical world that, to this point, has been quite dry to you. You are a beautiful warrior who is coming into their own. It is coming dear one. Hold on, the greater the burden, the greater the calling. Your burden has not been light. You have been well tested, but remember, I am always here to lighten your burden. I love you so much.

You are

Mysterious #27

Enigmatic, intriguing, and not easily understood, often drawing curiosity and fascination.

You are **Mysterious**

Hello sweetheart, this is it. Get ready! This is the time. You are, and will be, a mystery to many, and that is okay. Self-commit, self-love, self-pour and the rest will soon come. There is lightness coming to wrap you up. Your brain is extraordinary. Soon you will know and see that. Do not fret my dear, more is coming. More gifts will be activated to shake any remaining shackles and to help free others as well.

You are
Different #28

Standing apart from the norm,
unique, and/or distinct.

You are **Different**

I know, sweetheart. I know it's painful. I know it hurts when you feel like others give up on or misunderstand you. The truth is, they often do. I will never give up on you, however, and there are others who won't give up on you either. I know you prefer truth telling and truly, I will only tell you truth. Many others don't understand you. You are truly different and unique. You are a bridge, my sweet love, that means many at the ends of the spectrums will be pierced by you, as well as many who walk in darkness. It won't always be like this, but for a time, it will. You will continue to feel misunderstood. Others may continue to let you down. It is a part of current humanity, and although there is still goodness, you may continue to feel misunderstood, chastised. Know that I know you and your pain. I know your soul and all it encompasses. There are so many destinies that align, that pour into each other, that hold each other, that protect and love each other. There is beauty coming. I know your sweet heart, dear one. Things aren't always as they seem, and that the narrow path, for you, isn't the same as everyone else. Know that you are so very loved. Keep holding onto faith. Keep leaning in...when your heart hurts, and when it's joyous, and every time in between. You're beautiful. You are a gift.

You are

A Beautiful Creation #29

Wonderfully and intentionally made for a unique and magnificent reason.

You are a Beautiful Creation

My dear one, please know you are a child of the Creator. You are loved beyond measure and highly protected. I know there are times that you don't feel that way, however. Life has been very heavy. I know you sometimes feel angry about life circumstances and I understand. Yell and scream. I can take it. I want all of you, all that you are. There are plans and Divine purpose that is unable to be known or understood at this time, but please know, I have never left your side. Know that when you grieve, I grieve. When you have sorrow, I have sorrow. You are my dear child, and I feel that pain as your Abba. You are wrapped in my arms always.

Continue to pray for and seek miraculous healing. Please know that death of the physical body, while so painful, is but a blink in reality. Eternal life is eternal, infallible, and most beautiful. I have prepared a place for you and those you love.

You are
Treasured #30

**Highly valued, deeply appreciated, and held dear
with great love and care.**

You are **Treasured**

Yes, my love, yes!! You are finally getting it! It's the opposite of what you have often felt...unloved, unwanted, unworthy. You felt blessed to have anyone walk beside you. Finally, finally, you see it! Your humor, your light, your uniqueness...all of it. Don't you see, you are the gift, you are the treasure. You finally have eyes to see!

I am so very proud of you. It is all of the things you thought were "wrong" with you...all the things you thought were too much or too little, or too odd. Those are the things you needed to understand and where you needed to be.

Watch the beauty come, love, watch it come! You are the treasure by the sea.

You are

My Dearest #31

A deep affection, love, or closeness.
A term of endearment.

You are My Dearest

Oh, my dearest, how exciting is what is about to unfold. Your life is nearly in full bloom and your butterfly structure is drying its wings before flight.

The cresting of the mountain is happening. It isn't so others can see you, but so you can see just where your skills and gifts are needed. It is a beautiful view by which will give you a glimpse of where you can serve humanity.

It is going to be so beautiful. You can feel it, but you still have no idea how magnificent, impactful, and glorious it will be. It's going to be beautiful, my love.

It's all coming together. You'll soon see. Keep taking steps, one at a time, where led. This isn't an easy path. This is the narrow road, the narrow gate, it is in trueness and authenticity that you reach the peak. Do you know what a gift, what a feeling it is to know something so amazing is going to happen? What a precious gift, my dearest!

YOU ARE ~ 40 days of Hope, Healing, and Love. Messages of Love to Encourage, Empower, and Inspire.

You are
Magnificent #32

Grand, exceptional, impressive,
and awe-inspiring.

You are **Magnificent**

Sweetheart, this is your time. Let it all crack open. Your wisdom. Your love. Your humor. Your light. Your experience. Your warmth. You, as a vessel. You are magnificent. Know this. Please, know this. Believe it to the core of your being.

It's time for you to put pen to paper, paint to canvas, notes to the lyrics, purpose to the path. Do this without any judgement of yourself. Be boundless. Flow like the river. Ride the rapids. It's time to create, to heal, to be a wise leader & teacher.

You are

Courage ~#33~

The ability to face fear, adversity, or
uncertainty with bravery and determination.

You are **Courage**

My sweet one, you are so very courageous. This isn't an easy journey. You are being asked to shake the foundations that you yourself have stood on. Put yourself out there. You will be judged harshly and you know this. Forge ahead anyway.

Your true north, simply, is my voice, and you know its tone. You know what the frequency of the Way is. Sing, write, dance, play, paint, teach. I am so very proud of you. You walk a road that few can. It will be difficult at times, but also so very rewarding. You are loved and you are love. You are my kin and my kind. I love you so, so very deeply. You are protected by many beautiful, trusted angels.

You are

A Leader #34

Someone who guides, inspires, and influences, with wisdom and vision, others toward a goal.

You are a Leader

Your path is different, my dear one. You realize how rigid and structured people believe life needs to be. You recognize differently. Freedom rests in the flow. You are a special type of leader, of healer, of wise one. You have vast knowledge within your soul. Your ability to teach and heal is endless because I am endless.

It is coming. The great shift is coming. For you, and for many. Help people heal and better love each other. Help them find purpose from pain, understand their misunderstanding, elevate all around you. Breathe it in and breathe it out, my love.

You are

Chosen #35

Selected for a special significant
path, purpose, or destiny.

You are **Chosen**

My sweet love, you are one in over 8 billion. I know, everyone is, but like all my precious ones, know you are golden, and rare, and you are so very loved. Your position in this place is about originality and authenticity, a fierce but tender-hearted warrior. It's about love above all. It's about being a strong parent and leader for so very many. It's about loving and bringing goodness, not detriment, to others. You are one meant to love others into awakening to their purpose calling. Your wishes have always been for others…to heal them, for them to feel loved & cared for. You are on this path to be an illuminator to many, to love them, and to show, boldly and proudly, what true love looks like. You truly want to see people shine, and to see joy. Keep bringing the light, tender and fierce, tenaciously full of love, peace, comfort and goodness. You will sail and rise.

You are

A Bridge #36

A connector between people, ideals, or paths, aiding others through transition or obstacles, a means to unity.

You are **a Bridge**

Hey there, sweet one!! You are a bridge, a hand holder, a vessel, a way-shower. You provide trusted and safe passage over rough and treacherous terrains and great bodies of water. You shine light in dark places. That is often why people respond to you in the way that they do. Some don't like the illumination of darkness. It can be painful and difficult, I know, but please know that there are those who love you very much. Many respond to you in hurtful ways. It's hard, but it's beautiful. There are not many who can truly take on the path of genuine healing. You are needed in this capacity. This is a hard path but have faith in the unfolding. Follow the leading in purpose, it all aligns and is all an interwoven tapestry. This is a time of shift, of being present, grateful, patient, and thoughtful. Trust. Trust, and receive.

You are

Prepared #37

Ready and equipped for challenges,
opportunities, or future events.

YOU ARE ~ 40 days of Hope, Healing, and Love. Messages of Love to Encourage, Empower, and Inspire.

You are **Prepared**

You have been training to be that fierce, kind place of safety for so many. My dear one, you still don't realize how rare true unconditional love is. You feel like your different is sometimes "bad", but that does not align with the truth. Do not be afraid to be fully in your genuine authenticity, fully who you were made to be. Drive ahead with truly you. You've been trained for what's coming since you were a little one. In the way of truly knowing pain, in learning to fluff, freeze, or run to survive. There is no more hiding. You are a leader. One who leads in the only true way...from the front, through fear, through adversity, through the unknown. You become more yourself with each passing day. Keep tearing down the walls. You are meant to lead, to lead with an unfiltered, unadulterated kind of love.

You are

Fierce #38

Bold, strong, and determined, showing fortitude, intensity, passion, and resilience.

You are **Fierce**

You carry a love that is soft and tender but also fierce, loyal, and ever-enduring. You are sweet and kind and joyful but are unwavering to the truth and its way of love. That is your true north, your guiding compass, and with that, you'll never falter. That is where you find it all. Keep wrapping others in your warm, safe, loving arms. Remember, until you breathe no more, it is never too late to help walk others home. To extend a hand from the wall. To step boldly through the unpaved.

You are

A Smile-Bringer #39

Someone who spreads happiness, positivity, and joy to others through their actions, words, and presence.

You are a Smile-Bringer

Sweetheart, the world needs more of that beautiful smile of yours. It truly heals. Your words are so powerful, but your smile and that quirky, sweet laugh of yours mends wounds as well. The love exude in a smile is often underrated. I know, truly, how one beautiful, genuine, caring smile can pull others from the ledge. Smiles have saved so many lives. It makes no matter if your teeth are straight or your smile is crooked, the medicine contained in a smile heals just the same. Simply showing love and care, laughing and smiling, has bested the end for many.

You are
Called #40

To be summoned or appointed.

You are Called

My dear one, you are called for such a time as this. You have been purposefully, intentionally, beautifully placed in, and on, this Earth. You are here with a mission of great importance. Do you think I would know the number of hairs on your head if it was not so? You are so very precious to me, and to this time on Earth. You are so very needed and necessary. Love in full bloom, sweet one. Love in full bloom.

My dear friend,

It is my interceding prayer and great hope that these messages wrap you in everlasting love and heal your innermost wounds. May the hands of grace and goodness touch every place in need of mending. May the voice that breathed life into your lungs replace, with love, every negative word or limiting belief. May you know fully that you are PRECIOUS, you are LOVED, you are CHOSEN, you are MORE THAN ENOUGH, and you are darn sure WORTHY of each and every miracle and wonder.

With love and thankfulness,

Dr. Britt Elizabeth is the author of this work. It is her fervent prayer that the messages shared through her work meet the reader in their place of need, bringing miraculous healing, love, hope, and a renewed passion for life. Britt is a Registered Nurse who holds a Doctorate in Nursing Practice. She is a Navy Veteran and Mom. She is called to love, share, and bridge peoples, missions, medicine, beliefs, and ideals. She is gifted in areas of prophetic exhortation, poetry, creative writing, teaching, and healing.

~ A special thank you to my mom, Beth, for her endless support of this work, numerous proofreads, and continued encouragement of its need for an audience and publication ~

www.ingramcontent.com/pod-product-compliance
Lightning Source LLC
Chambersburg PA
CBHW060415050426
42449CB00009B/1973